CW00405254

Managing
Aggression
Course Book

OTHER PUBLICATIONS IN THE SERIES:

For information on this or other courses please contact:

LEARN CARE EXCEL

Matthews House
21 Thorley Park Road
Bishops Stortford
CM23 3NG

Tel: 07774 880880

info@learncareexcel.co.uk
www.learncareexcel.co.uk

Contents

INTRODUCTION

Many people enter the care industry because they have a desire to do just that: CARE. So, often people are unprepared for the stark reality of what is actually involved in caring for someone and must go through a rapid learning curve in terms of adjusting to trials that they may have to face on a daily basis. This adjustment may be triggered by something as harmless as a lack of awareness as to how much "paper-work" is involved in looking after the elderly but could equally come about when a worker is confronted by a level of aggression that leaves them frightened and unsure about what to do.

This text aims to help workers in the care industry understand what causes aggression, both in the people they are looking after and their colleagues, as well as how best to deal with it when it does surface.

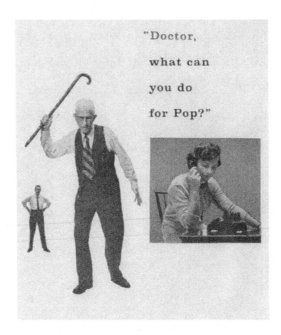

As with all the texts in this series, information in this course book is aimed at workers in the care industry and discussion will concentrate particularly on adults in these settings. If you are supporting younger people or people with specific needs please consult further texts.

Aggression
/ əˈɡrɛʃ(ə)n/

Noun – hostile or violent behaviour; readiness to attack or confront, with or without provocation; forcefulness; bullying.

synonyms: Hostility, antagonism, belligerence, truculence, assertiveness, audacity, boldness, rudeness, brashness, dominance, control.

The Health and Safety Executive defines aggression in the work place as *"any incident in which a person is abused, threatened or assaulted in circumstances relating to their work,"*[1] For the care worker this definition includes:

- Cared for people: no matter in what capacity they assist the person
- Colleagues: there may be many circumstances when a worker may experience or witness an outburst
- Themselves: care workers are not exempt from experiencing aggression and it is just as important to understand how to manage and control these feelings.

Aggression in the work place can manifest in many ways, ranging from physical attacks, which pose immediate risk of injury, to prolonged verbal abuse, which can lead to long term health implications for the victim.

Aggression can also have further impact on the work place as a whole and the HSE points out that aggression in the work place can lead to poor morale, a bad reputation for the organisation, difficulty in recruiting and keeping staff, increased absenteeism, and distress, anxiety, stress, injury and even disability or death among the work force. So, both employers and employees should be concerned to manage and reduce the threat of violence for the mutual benefit of each other.

---

[1] Source: www.hse.gov.uk

WHY IS AGGRESSION SO BAD?

Health. While there are circumstances in which aggression and anger can be useful, particularly if they are well managed and short lived, prolonged or excessive aggression and anger can have serious implications on a person's health due to effects such as raised blood pressure and stress levels.

Escalation. If a person expresses their anger through violent outburst these may trigger others to become defensive and angry as well. Sometimes this will escalate into violence

Reputation. The way in which we talk to others can also cause distress and hhaving a "short fuse" or a "vicious temper" can also damage a person's reputation or alienate them from those around them leading to social isolation.

FORMS OF AGGRESSION

Everyone experiences aggression in their own way. How quick they are to anger, how often they act out, how long it lasts, how intensely it is felt is all down to the individual and will vary throughout different times in their lives.

Equally the way we experience and express our aggression varies from person to person and throughout their life. Here are some of the forms that aggression can take:

Behavioural

- aggressive or cruel physical actions
- trouble making, defiance, acting out

Verbal

- aggressive or cruel words
- spreading rumours or false accusations

Passive

- mockery, evasion, refusal to co-operate
- avoid confronation when expressing anger

Self-Inflicted

- anger aimed inwardly
- includes starving and self harm

Chronic

- seems to be constantly angry with everything for particular reason - habit or disposition

Judgemental

- hurtful language used against people around
- belittling people or their abilities

Overwhelmed
- anger at the entire situation
- acting out to relieve frustration

Constructive
- anger that can be channelled into useful action

Volatile
- quick to come and quick to dissipate
- may be explosive or mild

Retaliatory
- anger as a response to another's anger

Paranoid
- irrationally based on jealousy, mistrust or intimidation of others

Deliberate
- used to gain control or power in a situation
- will escalate if they do not get what they want

Intimidatory

- often manifesting as "the silent treatment"
- sometimes unintentional as the person withdraws within themselves to deal with an issue

Bullying

- umbrella category for prolonged intimidation, threats of violence or to reputation, isolation, overwork, destablising, prejudice and singling out for ridicule or harsh treatment

Violent

- the threat of or actual use of physical force which will likely cause injury or psychological damage
- It may be self-inflicted, such as self harm or starvtion
- It may be interpersonal (between people) in a aggressor / victim relationship and includes physical attacks, rape and unncesessay restraint
- It may be verbal and include things such as swearing, insults and racism

As can be seen above the list of types of aggression is very long and as already stated people can experience all of these types of aggression, both from others and themselves, at various times in their lives and often a combination of some together, and they can experience these for many, many reasons.

WHO CAN SHOW AGGRESSION?

As mentioned in the previous section, nobody is exempt to experiencing aggression, both in themselves and from others.

Aggression from Looked After People and Their Families

Even when everything is running smoothly, entering a home can be a very stressful situation for the person in need of care as well as their families. It can be shameful and frustrating for people who were previously independent to have to rely on others for help. It can be upsetting for families to admit they are no longer able to care for their loved ones. There are new surroundings, unfamiliar routines and even distances from their support network to adjust to. The list of emotions that people go through when entering a home or putting a loved one in a home is endless and unique to the individual. And that is when everything runs smoothly.

There may be issues around funding, or paperwork. There may be disagreements between family members. There may be a myriad of unforeseen things that cause delay, miscommunication or other problems. And all of these situations can cause a person's emotions to bubble up and erupt in anger and aggression.

Additionally, the cared for person may have additional issues such as Dementia or Alzheimer's where angry outbursts often accompany their condition.

Aggression from Colleagues

It is fair to say that the care industry can be extremely frustrating at times. Staff are often stretched to their limits and frequently low paid meaning that they might have struggles in their home life. These pressures may manifest in aggressive outbursts against residents and their families, fellow colleagues, managers and even suppliers and contractors.

Aggression from Managers

Just as workers in a care home, managers can experience a great deal of pressure both in the work place and in their own home. While it is particularly expected that managers will maintain a level of professionalism, they are still human and may find times when controlling their frustration and anger becomes difficult.

Aggression from the Public

When looking at care-home and care-in-the-home set ups there may be times when carers may have to deal with angry members of the public. This could be suppliers that are annoyed that they have to wait to see a manager before they can deliver their goods to neighbours of the care home complaining about visitors parking over their drive.

Aggression from Inside

Finally it must not be overlooked that we are all capable of "losing it" from time to time. Pressures at work and home and frustrations in dealing with these pressures can boil up and if we do not deal with them constructively they can spill out in unexpected and possibly damaging ways.

> IN EFFECT, AGGRESSION CAN AFFECT ANYONE AT ANY TIME
> THE KEY IS TO STOP IT BEFORE IT BECOMES A PROBLEM

CAUSES OF AGGRESSION

As well as understanding who may be affected by aggression it is also important to understand possible causes of this aggression.

Anger

Anger is a basic human emotion that everyone experiences at one time or another and it can be useful in that it is the way our minds tell us that something is wrong with a particular situation – when something is unfair, when someone has wronged us or when we face barriers to our goals. The emotions we experience when we are angry can help spur us into action, or can help our brain come up with novel solutions to our problems, or even just make us realise that something is wrong and needs our attention. But they can also become a problem in their own right, erupting from us as verbal or physical outbursts that are damaging, or causing us to develop dangerous opinions and prejudices and stop considering the feelings and position of others. Further, these sorts of outbursts can have a negative effect on those around us, escalating things and causing the situation to become even worse.

Stress

Modern living can be very stressful and working in the care industry can add its own set of stresses on top of that so it is not wonder that excessive stress is common among care workers. There are many ways that the body can let us know that we are experiencing stress and one of those is a loss of control over our emotions including the potential to act aggressively.

Fear

Fear can initiate instinctive responses from us and a common one of those is anger. It does not need to be a sudden incident that causes the fear but could be a growing dread from a situation that evolves slowly.

Lack of Control

Often we can feel helpless and unsure of where to turn and, as modern life can put multiple pressures on us, we can be left unsure how we are going to be able to cope. Pressures come from having to look after our family, children, partners and parents, keep up with our bills, and prepare for our future, to name a few. The frustration which comes from not being able to control or manage our lives can sometimes leak out in the form of aggression.

Bullying

Bullies are people who, for whatever reason, feel the need to control others. Often they do this through manipulation but sometimes they will use intimidation and the threat of, or actual, violence. Bullies are usually people with their own set of issues but who take these out on others.

Low Self-Esteem

Similar to bullies, people with low self-esteem usually have a set of underlying issues that can often mean they regard their own feelings as unimportant and can be easily manipulated by others. This leads to them being seen as an "easy touch" and given less consideration than others. Occasionally the situation can build up, however, and all the feelings that had previously been oppressed (that the person did not feel worthy to express) spill out in anger and aggression.

Bad Past Experiences

Sometimes a memory of a particular event can trigger an almost instinctive response and when the event was a bad one our minds will often go into instinctive modes of behaviour such as "fight or flight". If the "fight" instinct is triggered it can make the person end up acting out aggressively even though they are not really sure why they are doing it.

Poor Behaviour Modelling

It is sad to admit but there will always be people who have had poor role models as examples of how to behave. Some of these people will, unfortunately, repeat these unsuitable behaviours. Aggression may be a learned behaviour that is not appropriate but the person may not have access to any better alternatives.

Over stepping boundaries

There is of course the times when someone does not intend to be aggressive but their behaviour is not welcome and, as a result, may appear to be so. Someone who comes too far into a person's "personal space", someone whose voice and mannerisms are loud and imposing, or even someone who is over helpful can come across as aggressive when that is the last thing they would wish to do.

Medical Condition

Finally, there are many conditions such as Alzheimer's and Dementia that are becoming more and more common as our population becomes older, and workers in the care industry are often at the front line of those dealing with the disease. A common symptom of sufferers of these conditions is aggressive behaviour. It must be remembered that these people cannot help this behaviour and it should be dealt with compassionately. More information on this can be found in our book *Dementia Care (09DC)*.

HOW TO HANDLE AGGRESSION

When it comes to handling aggression there are two sides of the issue to tackle; when people are aggressive to us and when we are aggressive to others.

ON THE RECEIVING END OF AGGRESSION …

When it comes to dealing with aggression from others having an understanding of what is causing the aggression is the first stage in handling the situation. The previous section discusses why various people may display aggression and it can clearly be seen that it comes in many forms, from many different people and for many reasons. When experiencing aggression from another it is important to calm down and try to work out what is causing their behaviour.

ANGER, FEAR AND LACK OF CONTROL

If a particular incident has caused a person to rant then a calm assessment of the situation can analyse where the problem is. This can then be addressed and either the aggressive person can be reassured that the issue is being dealt with or they can be given an explanation as to why it is not possible to do any more than has already been done. Sometimes showing empathy and just letting the person know that you <u>hear</u> them can be enough to defuse the tension, allowing a practical solution to be found. Either way, it is essential to remain unruffled and it may be necessary to remind the person that being aggressive will achieve nothing. When something is wrong the best way to deal with it is to keep a cool head and take measured action.

This approach is also useful when someone is aggressive as a result of their fear in a particular circumstance or if they feel that they are losing control of their situation. Again, it is important to remain composed, assess the issue the person has and offer reassurance or practical support as necessary.

BULLYING, POOR BEHAVIOUR MODELLING AND OVERSTEPPING BOUNDARIES

Generally, bullies and badly behaved people have "learned" their behaviour as a way of achieving their desired goals; getting what they want. This is not to say that "what they want" is necessarily related in any way to what it is that they are being aggressive about.

A bully, for instance, "wants" to feel better about themselves or wants to make up for things that are happening elsewhere in their life. Often we can find ourselves going along with the overbearing, aggressive, even threatening behaviour, just for "an easy life" but it is extremely rare that this approach will be the best in the long run. As tolerating bullying behaviour usually does not provide the bully with what it is that they are actually trying to achieve, the bully can escalate, defeating the purpose of going along with the behaviour in the first place.

Equally, if someone who has developed poor modes of behaviour through inappropriate role modelling or has less than scrupulous morals, looking beyond the apparent issue can help you understand the actual motivation behind their aggression. Discovering and dealing with these issues can be very difficult and may mean several attempts at understanding the route cause and finding a way of working with these people.

In these situations the most important thing is to stand firm and show that you refuse to be treated inappropriately. Firstly, aggression must not be met with aggression but strength can be displayed in many more subtle ways. Secondly, communication is key to letting the aggressor know that, while you will not be intimidated or manipulated by them, if they adjust their behaviour everyone will be able to work together better.

STRESS

Dealing with aggression from someone who is stressed can be one of the hardest to deal with. Usually if their stress has got to a point where they are prone to aggressive outbursts they are suffering a great deal. It is often said that a little bit of stress is a useful thing in that it focuses the mind to deal with a situation but prolonged stress is very unhealthy and unhelpful and when a person who is stressed has got to the point that they are having frequent, disproportional eruptions the chances are that they need help in more areas than just the one that has caused the outburst. In these cases it can be useful to offer more assistance generally or, where appropriate, suggest that the person gets advice from professionals who can help. Be aware that many people do not wish to hear this advice so it will depend on the relationship you have with the stressed person as to how you approach them.

MEDICAL CONDITION

One of the primary places that a care worker will experience aggression is in dealing with their patience. Some will fall into the categories already mentioned above but many will fall into a group which is distinct and needs special consideration. This is the group who are suffering medical conditions which affect their mood, memory and conduct. The most important thing to remember when dealing with people in these situations is that they cannot help how they behave and extra patience is required when dealing with them. Sometimes just understanding this fact is enough to stop the aggression (or other harmful behaviours) from causing offense or injury but there are more techniques which can be utilised to assist. Some of these will be explored below but if you seek a greater understanding of these conditions please see our *Dementia Care (09DC)* text.

There are many ways that a carer can help to defuse a situation or even prevent it from happening in the first place. Some of these have already been discussed above and include things such as understanding a person's background or taking the time to listen. But there are many other ways that they can help.

Before taking steps to manage aggression it is vital to understand two things:

1. The **cause** of the aggression
2. The **trigger** of the aggression

In the previous section we have discussed several causes for aggression such as frustration, fear or underlying medical conditions.   If a carer understands these causes there are many things that can be done to address them before they become an issue. For instance, giving someone bad news may make them angry. Considering how they are informed of this may help reduce some of the anger, or giving them time and space to calm down may mean that they won't lash out and cause damage with their anger.

The causes of aggression themselves, however, will not cause necessarily aggressive behaviour. Sometimes, in order for the aggression to surface, there will need to be a trigger. Again, if a carer gets to know what a person's triggers are there may be things that could be done to manage the behaviour. For instance, if something a person has been looking forward to might be cancelled, give them as much notice as possible to help them feel in control of the situation.

Triggers include events such as:

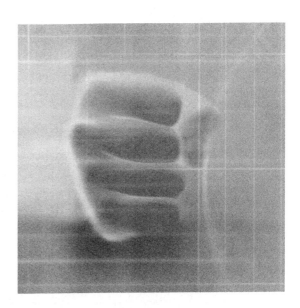

- Being made to wait
- Lateness
- Loud noises
- Insults
- Lack of choice
- Being spoken to like a child
- Not being informed about what is going on
- Frequent changes in staff
- Inappropriate medication
- Being cooped up inside
- Bad news from home
- Losing something

Carers should also be aware that from time to time people are subconsciously "looking for" a reason to be angry and will react at very minor or seemingly irrelevant triggers. In these cases it is important to go back to the previous step and consider the actual cause of the aggression and address it accordingly.

Calming Down

The next, most important step in managing aggression in others is to try to keep situations as calm as possible. If someone has already become aggressive this should be a priority as it is impossible to reason with someone when they are in this state and, unless they can be reasoned with, their problem cannot be resolved.

The steps to getting someone to calm down generally follow this pattern (although this is a very loose pattern and can easily be adjusted if required):

- Without being confrontational remind the person that aggression won't help
- Ask the person to sit down and offer them a drink of water or a cup of tea
- Stay positive in both attitude and body language (see the next section)
- Invite them to have a conversation about what has happened
- Show respect and empathy by listening to them and using their preferred name where appropriate
- Offer them reassurance, advice or give them space as is appropriate

During this process it is important not to invade the person's personal space as this can seem intimidating and, if they are already agitated, feeling uncomfortable (or even violated) will only escalate the situation. Remember the old adage "at arm's length" and this will generally be sufficient although getting closer can be acceptable if, for instance, you are beside rather than in front or you are assisting them to their seat, say.

Time to Reflect

Once the person is calm and the situation resolved it is important to give them time to think over their actions. This may mean that they need to be advised that their behaviour is not acceptable or it could mean suggesting alternative ways that they could deal with the situation in the future

Avoid Breakdown in Communication

As you can see from the chart below what we say makes up only a small part of our communication. With that in mind it is essential to ensure that what we say is as clear as possible.

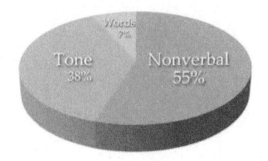

- In addition to understanding the reasons behind a person's anger it is useful to understand their cultural background
- The carer should speak clearly and loud enough for the person to hear without shouting, yawning, covering the mouth etc. And always use an even tone when speaking
- The carer should always be clear and specific in their instructions but never talk down to anyone
- The person should be given an opportunity to respond and the carer should ensure they listen to them.
- Do no talk over people
- Never gossip

Body Language

Our body language is a combination of our facial expressions, how we stand, body gestures, what we wear and even what we do when we are not actively trying to communicate. The thing to remember about body language is that it says far more than we ever could, or would even want to, say verbally. It gives the biggest clue as to how we are really feeling as we can <u>say</u> that we are happy even though we aren't, or we can <u>say</u> we understand even though we don't. Our body language will give us away. This form of nonverbal communication is very important as to how a person is portrayed as failure to communicate may lead to frustration and, in turn, aggression or violence.

Even though this lady says the same thing in both pictures the mean is very different in each case as her body language portrays.

I'm happy to help…

I'm happy to help…

Obviously we cannot help how we feel, and as long as we are professional, how we feel should never effect our work but we are only human and our body language can often "leak" what we truly feel. The good news is that the more we try to keep our body language positive, the better we will feel so it will become easier to do this. However only use movements and gestures that feel comfortable, as awkward gestures may send out the wrong signals. This leads to miss-read communication and can lead further to a failure to communicate. Just relax and be yourself.

Remember to be aware that:
ALTHOUGH BODY LANGUAGE IS A MAJOR FORM OF COMMUNICATION
SOME PEOPLE WILL SEE ONLY WHAT THEY WANT TO SEE

The table below includes examples of positive and negative body language:

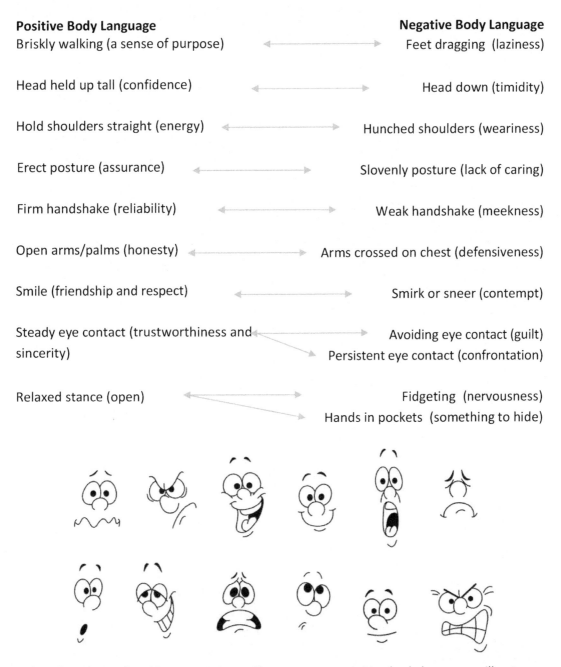

Positive Body Language	**Negative Body Language**
Briskly walking (a sense of purpose)	Feet dragging (laziness)
Head held up tall (confidence)	Head down (timidity)
Hold shoulders straight (energy)	Hunched shoulders (weariness)
Erect posture (assurance)	Slovenly posture (lack of caring)
Firm handshake (reliability)	Weak handshake (meekness)
Open arms/palms (honesty)	Arms crossed on chest (defensiveness)
Smile (friendship and respect)	Smirk or sneer (contempt)
Steady eye contact (trustworthiness and sincerity)	Avoiding eye contact (guilt)
	Persistent eye contact (confrontation)
Relaxed stance (open)	Fidgeting (nervousness)
	Hands in pockets (something to hide)

As already suggested making a conscious effort to portray positive body language will not only improve the mood of those around you, it will also help you to feel better about yourself and what you are doing. There are many techniques that can help a person learn to improve their body language but the most important thing is to relax and be yourself. It will also help to make life easier as up to 93% of our communication is made through our body language and making sure we are aware of how our body language is coming across (and making any adjustments necessary) can help make the whole process of communication easier.

Start with a smile. A genuine smile can help to lift the mood of any situation, offering reassurance, empathy and trust. Make sure that you greet everyone with a smile to start things off on the right foot.

Respect personal space. As already discussed the fastest way to make someone feel uncomfortable is to invade their personal space. Be conscious not to get too close or crowd someone.

Pay attention. If someone doesn't feel that they have your full attention they won't feel valued or that you have time or respect for them. Don't fiddle with objects, check your phone or be distracted while someone is talking to you.

Listen. Give the person you are speaking with the chance to have their say. Don't hog the conversation. Take turns talking and listening.

Look them in the eye. Keeping good eye contact (without starring) will show someone that you are interested in what they have to say.

Touch is a touchy subject. Some people are more tactile than others and appreciate the occasional touch on the arm or shoulder but not everyone feels this way so it is important to get to know the person first. For instance if they touch you in this way first, it is likely you can do the same.

Allow people (and yourself) privacy. Asking for (or giving) too much information, too early getting or too friendly too fast can make people feel uncomfortable.

Let people speak for themselves. People can be upset if someone speaks for them over their head, or finishes their sentence for them, or interrupts their story to tell one of their own. Listen and let them finish.

Think about how you look. While listening to someone be very conscious of your own facial expressions. Mirroring the other person's facial expressions shows interest.

People being bullied can experience anxiety, headaches, sleeplessness, tearfulness, loss of self-confidence, and even contemplate suicide, not to mention experiencing a myriad of stress-related illnesses, and the potential loss of pay from time off work. Workers who are experiencing bullying are under a great deal of stress and, consequently, will not be as productive in the work place as they could be. Stress must be dealt with in the same way as any other health and safety issues.

Bullying in the workplace occurs when someone is singled out for unfair treatment by a manager or colleague. Employers have a duty under the Health and Safety at Work Act 1974 to ensure the health, safety and welfare of their employees and this includes protection from bullying. Not ensuring this is done is not only a breach of an individual's contract of employment it is also breaking the law. Depending on the type of bullying there may also be a breach of sexual harassment and racial discrimination legislation as well as the Criminal Justice and Public Order Act 1994. Employers may face fines, claims for compensation and possibly a jail sentence alongside the bully. If bullying is not dealt with appropriately companies will experience a cost in terms of absenteeism and reduced productivity, poor morale, high staff turnover and even be faced with legal or tribunal proceedings, causing reputational damage.

Bullying is an umbrella term to cover negative actions such as harassment, intimidation, racism, discrimination and violence. Conflict will often occur in a work place as we are all individuals with our own opinions but it does not need to manifest into intimidating or bullying behavior, regardless of the power relationship of the people involved. Bullying is never acceptable, regardless of where it takes place and not just the workplace.

In the workplace, however, bullying can have a serious effect on the workforce and is acknowledged as one of the main causes of absenteeism. But the effects of bullying can stay with a person throughout their life and all cases that are reported should be investigated thoroughly and records kept of all incidents and the outcomes.

There is no comprehensive list of bullying behaviours but it tends to fall into five categories:
1. **Threat to professional status.** For example persistent attempt to belittle and undermine work or threats of disciplinary action without good cause
2. **Threat to personal standing.** Undermining personal integrity, using harmful innuendo, sarcasm, spreading rumours, forceful language or verbal threats.
3. **Isolation.** Withholding necessary information freezing out, ignoring, excluding
4. **Overwork.** Undue pressure, impossible deadlines, unachievable goals.
5. **Destabilisation.** "Moving the goal post" without consultation, persistent undervaluing efforts, or remove areas of responsibility without consultation

Being bullied, particularly at work, is a dreadfully demoralising and upsetting and no one should have to put up with it. But there are things that can be done.

Speak to the bully. The first step is to speak to the bully. Though it may be difficult a direct approach is usually the best. The bully must be told that their behaviour unacceptable and that it should stop. This is sometimes all that is needed. Bullies do not like being confronted particularly by someone who is calm and civilised.

Bullies will generally hide their activities so it is important to tell a friend or colleague. The chances are that more than one member of staff is being bullied and speaking to others will not only help to understand the extent of the problem but also provide support.

Keep a diary. In the same way, keeping a diary of incidents can help understand the pattern of behaviours that can be informative. It will provide a vital record of the nature of the bullying and timings. This is important because viewed in isolation many of the incidents may appear trivial but when viewed as a whole the pattern emerges. It may be important when confronting the bully.

Tell a manager or supervisor. Assuming it is not actually a manager who is doing the bullying then the next step is to inform a direct manager. The diary can be used to demonstrate the case. Take your diary with you to back up what you have to say. They may not believe it but by informing them, at least they have been officially told. The more people that know, the more difficult it is for the bully to flourish. If it is the direct manager who is doing the bullying, then their manager must be informed.

Ultimately, there may need to be a formal complaint but this is a serious step and must be treated as such. Never go to a meeting connected with the complaint without your union rep or a friend as a witness.

Unions. Representatives from a Union can be a great source of knowledge and support. Everyone's aim will be to stop the bullying quickly and quietly and the Union will work towards that by providing legal support and representation. Everyone has a right to join a union. Employers do not need to be informed, but if they find out, it is illegal for them to treat an employee unfairly as a result.

The Law. Workplace bullying, whilst common-place, is illegal and action can be taken under the following laws:

The Health and Safety at Work Act 1974 - imposes a legal duty on employers to look after the health, safety and welfare of their employees so far as is reasonably possible.

The Race Relations Act 1976 and The Race Relations (Amendment) Act 2000 may be used in cases of race discrimination which is defined as any unfair treatment aimed at a person because of race, colour, nationality, citizenship or ethnic origin or where there is hostile or offensive behaviour which is at least partially motivated by racial factors. The abuse may be either direct or indirect which occurs when a universal requirement puts people of a particular race at a disadvantage, such as a ban on head scarves.

The Sex Discrimination Act 1975 prohibits discrimination on the basis of a person's gender or marital status and under *The Employment Equality Regulations 2003* it is illegal for employers to discriminate due to sexual orientation. This also covers sexual harassment which is unwelcome behaviour of a sexual nature whilst in the course of employment.

Constructive Dismissal. An employee who is forced to resign because of unacceptable working conditions, including workplace bullying, may be the victim of constructive dismissal and entitled to claim compensation in the Employment Tribunal. Anyone who finds their working conditions unacceptable and believes they would have a case if they were to resign should seek urgent legal advice before taking any action.

To reiterate it is in everyone's interest to eradicate bullying from the work place and this is because of the toll it takes on the people being bullied but also the work place as a whole.

AGGRESSION FROM WITHIN...

Much of this text so far has been to cover what happens when someone experiences aggression from others or witnesses it occurring but it is vital not to neglect the potential of aggressive behaviour within ourselves as this can happen very easily.

In order to understand where this aggression may come from it is useful to understand ourselves. Many things may affect how we behave in a certain situation because these things make up who we are and what we have experienced throughout our lives, which in turn affects how we react in certain situations. The things that make us who we are include our:

- Gender
- Ethnicity and nationality
- Personality, for instance how outgoing or shy we are
- Religion
- Politics
- Family, for instance how anger was dealt with in the home

We may have had bad experiences in relation to any of the above which may put us on our guard or even make us oversensitive to certain situations that we come across in the work place. Conversely, we may not have experienced any of the dreadful things that others may have gone through in which case we need to show more sensitivity than we would do for ourselves.

Other factors may have a more immediate effect on how we behave. For instance, we may have family or money worries that distract us and mean that we do not do our job properly or take our frustration out on the clients or colleagues in a care home. Alternatively, as a carer some people may see you as invasive or controlling, while you are just trying to help them and do your job. While it is important to show an appropriate level of authority in these situations it can become frustrating when the people we are supposed to look after make it difficult for us to help them.

Nobody is perfect but as long as we try our best to remain patient and not to let things get the better of us, that we accept that we make mistakes and take responsibility for those, rather than trying to blame others, and that we do our best to improve ourselves, everyone will benefit, not least ourselves.

> We usually don't mean to do or say anything to annoy or upset anyone and think we are not to blame for others aggressive behaviour but in some cases this is not true.
>
> By just looking closer at ourselves and our behaviour we may find the answer.

Step One

As stated above the most important thing when managing our own behaviour is to get to know ourselves. What makes us tick, how we react in certain situations and how we can manage and improve our behaviour.

The next most important thing is to remember to be patient, particularly with those who, for whatever reason, cannot control their aggression. This could be the clients we look after who have dementia or their family member who have just had some bad news. It could be our colleagues who are having difficulty at home or a delivery man who is under pressure from his boss. Patience and remaining calm is the best way to deal with these situations.

We all experience anger and aggression in our own unique way so if we learn to understand our own style we can learn to control it, or even turn it into something positive. Learning about our own behaviour requires a conscious effort to become aware of our actions and feelings (because they are automatic the rest of the time).

- Look out for signs that your frustration is building, for instance, grinding teeth or becoming annoyed with something you normally don't mind.
- Try to find out exactly what it is that is bothering you – often it is not the thing that you are taking your frustrations out on
- Keep a diary to help you identify if there are any patterns or recurring triggers (such as "Monday mornings" or a pushy boss
- Make a note of the behaviours that are inappropriate (such as raising your voice, storming off, nasty comments – don't worry, we all do them)
- Make a note of the consequences of your behaviour as this will act as a benchmark to measure your improvement as well as offer inspiration for what to aim for
- Consider whether there are any underlying issues or emotions that may be contributing to the aggression (such as depression, stress from family and so on)

Step Two

Once you have examined the possible underlying causes of aggression you can look at ways of tackling it. First it is important to find ways to calm down. This could be a "time-out" when you see the signs of anger start to emerge. This might be removing yourself from the situation for a time (make sure you let others know what you are doing so they don't think you are "storming off") or taking a deep breath or counting to ten.

It is important to give yourself time to think before you act as acting on an angry impulse is rarely good. If you have difficulty interrupting or stopping this anger you could try these other "calming down" techniques:

- Recognising that just because you <u>are</u> angry, doesn't mean you have to <u>act</u> angry
- Avoid reacting on impulse. Even though you feel like lashing out this will only make things worse in the long run. If you cannot think of something else to do, do nothing.
- Don't tackle aggression in others. Responding to someone else's aggression is like a reward for their bad behaviour. Don't respond to outbursts or walk away if that is difficult and inform them that you will discuss it with them when they are feeling calmer
- Practice some calming phrases such as "life's too short" or "calm down" or "take a breath" that you can say quietly to yourself or simply tell yourself to "stop" when you notice you are becoming angry
- Visualise a calming scene and imagine yourself there

Calming down or telling yourself to stop is not suppressing your anger but, rather, taking charge of it. You are making the decision not to allow your anger to escalate and do harm and giving yourself the opportunity to tackle your anger in a different way.

Step Three

The next step in tackling aggressive behaviour is to model and practice more appropriate responses. Visualise alternative ways to handle the situation or take examples from others who you have witnessed handling the situation better than you.   Try to find positives in any situation as well as positive ways to behave. The more you practice this step the better you will become at it until it becomes second nature to you and your old ways of reacting seem strange to you.

You may also need to learn to assert yourself as a way of tackling the cause of your frustration. It may mean talking to the person who is making you feel upset or it may mean standing up for yourself.   You could even channel some of the anger you feel to give you the strength to do this. Be sure not to let it become a personal attack and stick to speaking about how you are feeling.   Again, the more you practice this, the easier it will become.

You could also consider developing a sense of humour about the issues to lighten the mood, seeking the help of others, or investigation activities that will help let out your frustration such as exercise, relaxation exercises or art. Avoid drinking alcohol or taking drugs, however, as a form of stress relief.

Just remember, everyone gets angry from time to time and everyone has the right to seek remedy. You are not a bad person for doing this but letting your anger control you will only have adverse effects on you and those around you. It is your responsibility to express yourself appropriately and their responsibility to do the same.

ON PAPER

As with all sections of the care industry, keeping up to date and accurate records of what is going on is essential to providing a great service. Subjects relating to aggression at work are no exception.

- There are many laws relating to aggression and violence in the work place (some of which have already been mentioned and more of which can be found in the last section of this text)
- Every home should have a policies and procedures document intended to deal with aggression and violence in the work place
- Detailed records should be kept about any incidents and, where required, these should be reported to the relevant authorities
- Risk assessment and care plans should be done to prepare for the possibility of aggression or violence from residents
- Finally, a culture of openness should be fostered so that anyone experiencing or witnessing aggression or violence can report the issue without fear of reprisal.

Informing others that their behavior is not acceptable can be distressing for all concerned so having proper procedures to help prevent the incidents from occurring in the first place, clear guidelines about what to do if it does and accurate records about what has occurred will help everyone feel reassured that the best is being done for all concerned.

RISK ASSESSMENT

The aim of a risk assessment is to find out the likelihood of events occurring. It is a vital tool in the work place and must be prepared and used properly. The principles of risk assessment remain the same regardless of the risk being assessed and when done in conjunction with the relevant legislation can help to provide a much better work environment, even save lives.

A risk assessment should follow these steps:

1. Look for hazards
2. Decide who is at risk from these hazards
3. Assess the comparative category of the risk
4. Record the findings
5. Assess the process and review as necessary

Categories of risk		
Low Only a slight chance of the event from occurring and minimal harm if it does	**Medium** High risk of occurring but minimal consequences Low risk of occurring but high consequences	**High** High risk of occurring and significant consequences

Policies and Procedures

Once a risk assessment has been carried out a plan of action can be set up. This will be included as part of the home's policies and procedures documents. It will involve describing what will happen in each circumstance, who is responsible for what role, what records must be kept and, more than likely, include details of how to lodge a grievance.

The Plan of Action should be implemented immediately and the outcomes checked to be sure that everyone is being looked after according to the legal (and moral) obligations. If any issue arise these should be rectified immediately also but there should be regular reviews in any case to be sure this document is up to date.

Record Keeping

It cannot be stressed enough how important it is to keep accurate and timely records. Details of how to keep records that are required by law will be included in the policies and procedures documents but the need to keep accurate records is also essential for individuals in a care home.

As cases of aggression and bullying are often hard to prove and memories and emotions become tangled together making a diary note of an event as soon as possible is sometimes the only proof that something has occurred and also the most accurate record of the details.

SUMMARY

Aggression in the work place is a very serious issue which can affect any one at any time and which can have serious consequences for everyone concerned. That is why it is important for everyone to be vigilant at all times and why they must act if they see it occurring while also striving to stop it occurring in themselves.

Sometimes it can be as simple as pointing out unacceptable behaviour to an individual or simply adjusting how we stand when we speak to people. But at others, serious action must be taken such as an Employment Tribunal, or even calling the police.

Everyone has a right to be free from the threat of or actual aggression in the work place and the law provides protection in this but eradication of this starts with the individual and so it is important for us all to be aware of this problem at all times and take steps to solve it when we see it in ourselves, receive it from others or witness it being done to someone else.

RELEVANT LEGISLATION & GUIDANCE

There are many regulations and laws that put a duty of care on workers as well give guidance on how best to look after health, safety and welfare in the work place. Some of these have been mentioned in previous sections but the full list of the ones which relate particularly to aggression in the work place are included here. More detailed information can be found Health and Safety Executive's *Violence at Work* leaflet or their website.

The Health and Safety at Work etc Act 1974 (HSW Act) Which puts a legal obligation on employers to ensure, so far as is reasonably practicable, the health, safety and welfare at work of their employees.

The Management of Health and Safety at Work Regulations 1999 Which states that employers must assess the risks to employees and make arrangements for their health and safety by effective:
- Planning
- Organization
- Control
- monitoring and review.

The risks covered should, where appropriate, include the need to protect employees from exposure to reasonably foreseeable violence.

The Reporting of Injuries, Diseases and Dangerous Occurrences Regulations 1995 (RIDDOR) Which makes it a requirement that employers must notify their enforcing authority in the event of an accident at work to any employee resulting in death, major injury or incapacity for normal work for three or more consecutive days. This includes any act of nonconsensual physical violence done to a person at work.

Safety Representatives and Safety Committees Regulations 1977 (a) and **The Health and Safety (Consultation with Employees) Regulations 1996** (b) Where employers must inform, and consult with, employees in good time on matters relating to their health and safety. Employee representatives, either appointed by recognised trade unions under (a) or elected under (b) may make representations to their employer on matters affecting the health and safety of those they represent. Effective management of

NHS and Community Care Act 1990 which requires social services to assess an individual's needs for living within the community. They should also provide clear procedures for complaints, comments, and registration and inspection requirements. Reviews of a person's ability to contribute should also be taken into consideration.

LEARN CARE EXCEL

Matthews House
21 Thorley Park Road
Bishops Stortford
CM23 3NG

Tel: 07774 880880

info@learncareexcel.co.uk
www.learncareexcel.co.uk

Printed in Great Britain
by Amazon

39737701R00020